Cat Club

Ragdolls

by Cameron L. Woodson

Bullfrog Books

Ideas for Parents and Teachers

Bullfrog Books let children practice reading informational text at the earliest reading levels. Repetition, familiar words, and photo labels support early readers.

Before Reading

- Discuss the cover photo. What does it tell them?
- Look at the picture glossary together. Read and discuss the words.

Read the Book

- "Walk" through the book and look at the photos. Let the child ask questions. Point out the photo labels.
- Read the book to the child, or have him or her read independently.

After Reading

- Prompt the child to think more. Ask: Ragdoll cats have light fur on their bodies and darker fur on their faces, ears, tails, and legs. Can you think of any other cat breeds with this coloring?

Bullfrog Books are published by Jump!
5357 Penn Avenue South
Minneapolis, MN 55419
www.jumplibrary.com

Library of Congress Cataloging-in-Publication Data

Names: Woodson, Cameron L., 1994– author.
Title: Ragdolls / Cameron L. Woodson.
Description: Minneapolis: Jump!, Inc., [2021] |
Series: Cat club | Includes index.
Audience: Ages 5–8 | Audience: Grades K–1
Identifiers: LCCN 2019049919 (print)
LCCN 2019049920 (ebook)
ISBN 9781645274537 (hardcover)
ISBN 9781645274544 (ebook)
Subjects: LCSH: Ragdoll cat—Juvenile literature.
Classification: LCC SF449.R34 W66 2021 (print)
LCC SF449.R34 (ebook)
DDC 636.8—dc23
LC record available at https://lccn.loc.gov/2019049919
LC ebook record available at
https://lccn.loc.gov/2019049920

Editors: Jenna Gleisner and Susanne Bushman
Designer: Jenna Casura

Photo Credits: cynoclub/Shutterstock, cover; Erik Lam/Shutterstock, 1, 14, 22; madeinitaly4k/Shutterstock, 3, 10; Tierfotoagentur/N. Noack/Age Fotostock, 4; Linn Currie/Shutterstock, 5 (foreground), 23tm; Africa Studio/Shutterstock, 5 (background), 8-9, 23tl; Cyndi Monaghan/Getty, 6–7; Serita Vossen/Shutterstock, 11, 23br; Ovia Images/Alamy, 12–13; COULANGES/Shutterstock, 15 (foreground), 23bl; Evgeniya Uvarova/Shutterstock, 15 (background), 23bl; Thomas Barwick/Getty, 16–17; dezy/Shutterstock, 18–19; Yellow Cat/Shutterstock, 18–19 (toy); JTSorrell/iStock, 20–21 (foreground), 23tr; ben bryant/Shutterstock, 20–21 (background), 23tr; Tennessee Witney/Shutterstock, 23bm; Eric Isselee/Shutterstock, 24.

Printed in the United States of America at Corporate Graphics in North Mankato, Minnesota.

Table of Contents

Soft Fur

This is a Ragdoll!

How did these cats get that name?

I pick mine up.
It goes limp.
Like a rag doll!

These cats can be big!

They are gentle.

They love to be with their owners.

Their fur is soft.
It is long.

It forms a ruff.

Their fur needs care.
We brush it each day!

brush

Most of their fur is light.
Their faces and ears are darker.

Their legs and tails can be darker, too!

We call this a point pattern.

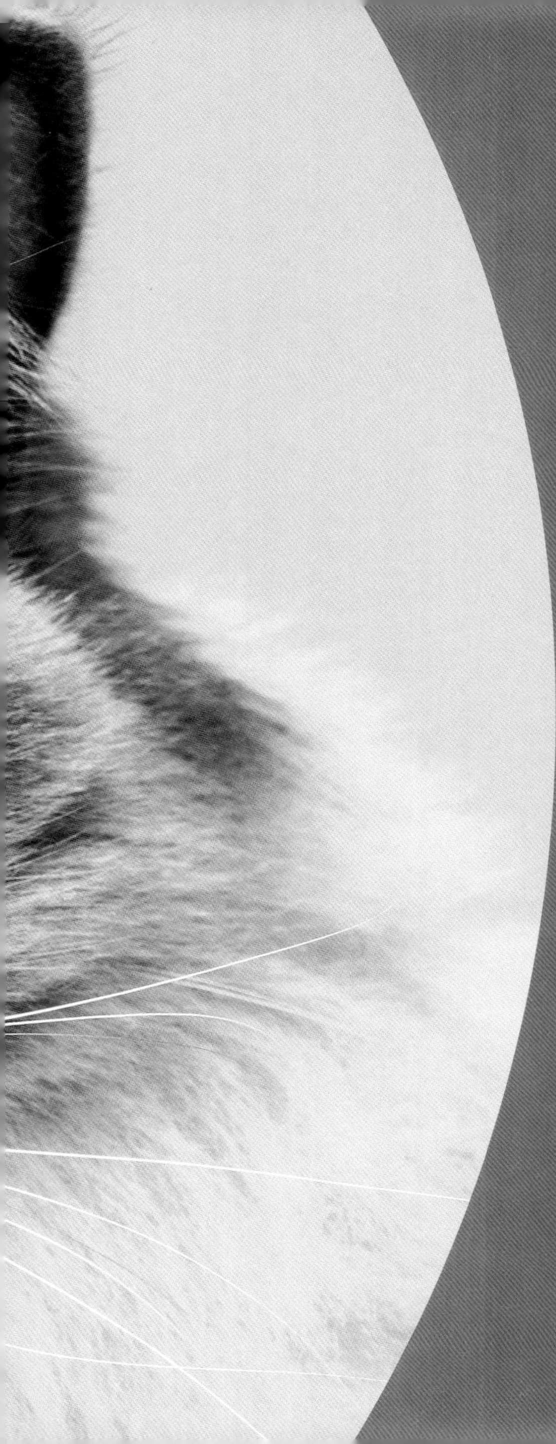

Their eyes are blue.

Pretty!

They love to play!

They do not like to be up high.

Ours chases toys on the floor.

toy

Would you like a Ragdoll?

A Ragdoll Up Close

A Ragdoll has blue eyes and long, soft fur that forms a ruff. Take a look at its other body parts!

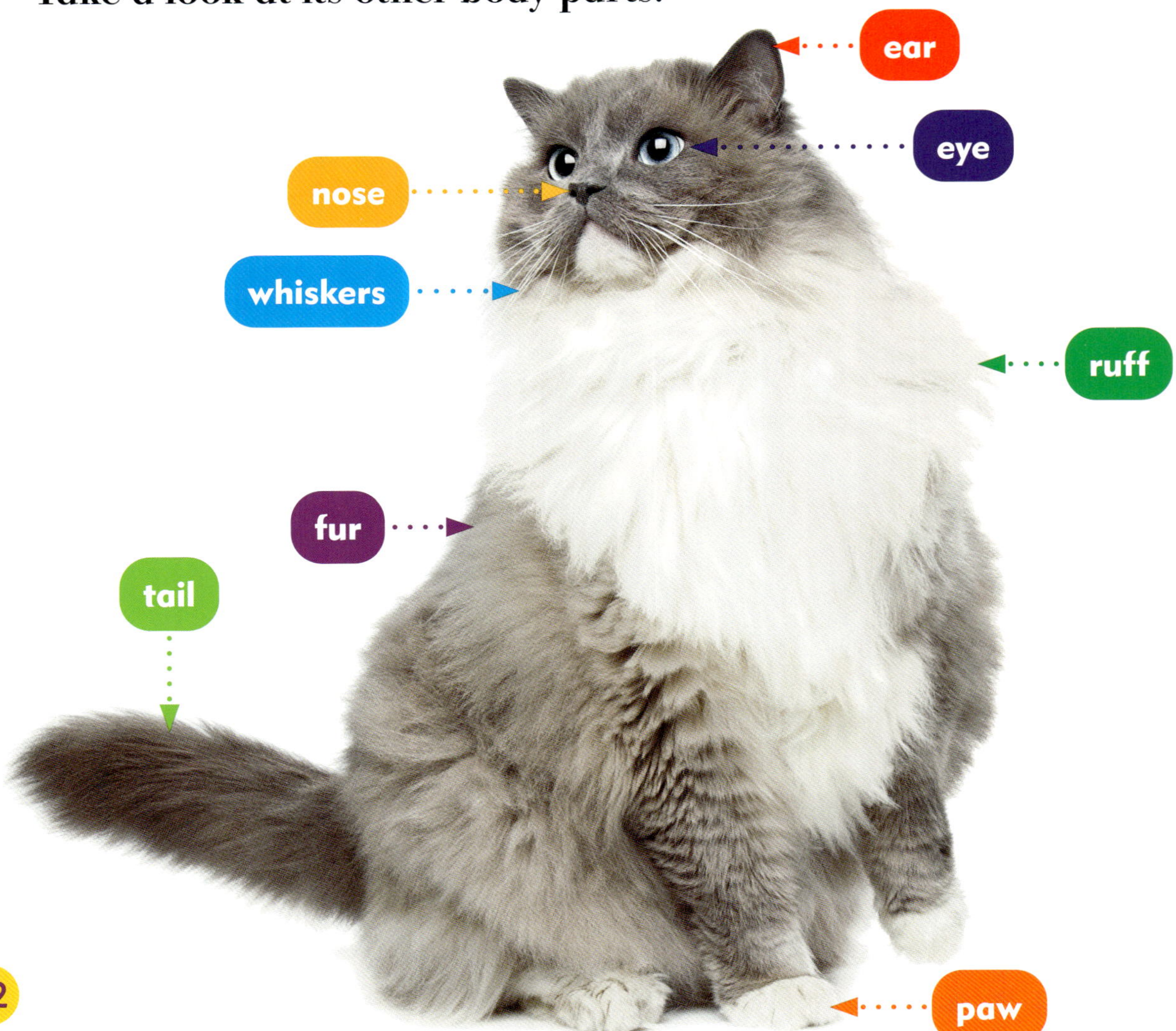

Picture Glossary

gentle
Not rough.

limp
Lacking strength or firmness.

owners
People who own pets.

point pattern
A color pattern in which fur on the face, tail, legs, and ears is darker.

rag doll
A soft, stuffed doll made of cloth.

ruff
A collar of fur.

Index

To Learn More

Finding more information is as easy as 1, 2, 3.

1. Go to www.factsurfer.com
2. Enter "Ragdolls" into the search box.
3. Click the "Surf" button to see a list of websites.